Mad Love, Praise and get
Drugged Cannons Whispe

MW00975215

"An amazing book to make you question your own outlook on life...this little book is without question, one of the best of its kind...I have read it over and over, each time picking up a new nugget to make me appreciate and question existence, all at the same time." – Troy Boyd, writer, poet, marketer

"...dips into just about anything and everything, and the effects are powerful...Mandella's little island is a world unto itself." – Blake Morrow, *Paperback Hit or Miss Weekly*

"A Freudian analysis chock full of neo-archaic allegories, pointed lyrics and secular prophecy." – William Keen, *Southeast Literary Review*

"A jazzy, at times, colorful improvement on ordinary speech...a ruthless, laconically efficient entertainment machine." – Mitchell Ross, *Under Cover Book Reviews*

"Mandella is possibly the rogue agent of Satan...ribald, reflective and versatile...the resilient dread results in a subtle, ingenious work." – Julia Spencer, *Omaha Chronicle*

"Is he clairvoyant or are the whisky soaked verses talking?" – Spencer Weston, *National Library Journal Review*

"Lurking beneath the rabidly funny, lies the strains of some of the finest chaotic and extraordinary tales of burning resentment I have yet to witness..." – Allen Mendenhall, *Kirkwood Publishers Weekly*

"...no conventional poetic or grammatical styles, but a very enjoyable read, nonetheless...some of the subject matter makes you squirm a bit, but it comes off as being honest and heartfelt." – Brent Lee, NYU literary major

And more pissing about...

"As subtle as a stick in the eye...very funny, but I think the guy (Mandella) does need some mental health attention...I will say, the one-liners are very original and witty...better than 95% of the slop I have read recently..." – James Roderick, *N.Y. Post Review*

"Some of the things the author comes up with border hilarity...some are down-right genius...recommended for its array of sardonic gestures that are seemingly incomprehensive to mere mortals..." – Tom Lorenzo, *Cleverly Artful Literary Press*

"...there is no tiptoeing around the seduction...Mandella is there to pillage...his style is peerless." – Alexandria Corsetti, author of *'When Shadows Conspire'*

KEITH A. MANDELLA

DRUGGED
CANNONS
WHISPER

Wasteland Press
Shelbyville, KY USA
www.wastelandpress.net

Drugged Cannons Whisper
By Keith A. Mandella

First Printing – September 2006
ISBN13: 978-1-60047-047-9
ISBN10: 1-60047-047-5
Back cover photo by Pilar Arevalo

Printed in the U.S.A.

FastForeWard

The mass-bulk of the content of Drugged Cannons Whisper was conceived and written between the summer of 1995 and winter of 1997. It was first published thru Watermark Press in early 1998.

The initial and only 2,500 copies were pressed and distributed at an alarming rate. They literally, uh huh, flew off the shelves. In a flash, they were gone...

Now an extreme rarity to find and sought after the world over, DCW is now an item of literary and humanitarian importance. Collectors, historians and the common folk alike have put up unprecedented and sometimes undisclosed amounts of lucre to obtain copies of the shrouded and almost near-unobtainable original pressing of DCW.

I was initially approached by the caretaking committee of the Library of Congress in the early loins of winter in 1999 to do a repress. Then, shortly after, the prophetic flood of various national and international poetic societies, the Writers Guild of New Zealand, members of the Maritime Journal of Literary Greats of Our Time and even my own organization, the Tongues Tourniquet Foundation, began their relentless pursuit of my approval.

At first, I was appalled at the mere thought of doing a second edition or re-press. I was stoutly reluctant mainly due to the fact that I believe in the integrity of a single and final book pressing. That is what makes a classic a classic and makes a collectors item, just that: a collector's item.

But money does indeed talk, as they say. And mine usually says, 'Goodbye!' Integrity, pride and optimism do not pay the bills. Royalties, readings and signings, however do.

FastForeWard (cont)

The reader (you) can only begin to feel the effects, intensity and sheer burden of the thought process the author (me) has subjected himself to and has had to endure;

- Irreplaceable layers of Sanity-
- Sporadic kidney dysfunction-
- Liver 'discrepancies'-
- Violent fits of torturous depression-
- Excessive and often unexplainable laughter-
- Riotous intoxication thru self medicating-

And serene bouts of tender, sweet nostalgia all contributed to getting to the 'Bottom of Things'…

Now breathe deep. Load your favorite cocktail tumbler with the correct octane booster or mood enhancer, and enjoy the squirming uneasiness of 'Drugged Cannons Whisper'. Again...for the very, first time.

Cheers!
Kam

Dedicated with unconditional love to my sister, Tanya.

CONTENTS

Abandoned

Stomping delicately on petals painted
Soaring briskly through ashes of burnt orchids tainted
Running my fingers over the soft, stone pollen
My glands numb and arid
Drought;
As if the phobia was now comforting...

To avenge this morbid flooding,
   I boycott the uteral canal tariffs

I wish I could be a fly of inertia...
You know the ones that bend suddenly south on tied bindings?
Harpoon addicts with lashing wit
   And ardent tongues,
Gondoliers with gonorrhea row defiantly on my daffodils
Despite constant wanting of curiosity maimed
Pelican's armada dealt on catacomb galleons
Celebrated whirlwinds and smoothing maroon abduction
Neural grace and nausea caused by rolling lucidity...
Feeding bundled exposure
Float with me...

I'm not the molar in your shoulder I claim to be
A twisted, speckled nautical enema breeds
   Rather quaint indulgences on your account
Incident gathering castrated pigmentation,
   Dull with imposing, overt confidence
I can only applaud your efforts if I can juggle your doubts-

Abandoned (cont)

The needlepoint sphere I crawl on;
The same halo I hallucinate and endorse
Do you support these erroneous efforts?

In dire need of lengthy appraisal;
Pushed into the world I carry in my pocket

How will I foreshadow denied tension?
Pellets of reason pelt on the brow of outrage...

Weave yourself back in;
For a moment I thought you got lost...
I lost you...
Abandoned.

Trouble with the Truth

Those crusty joints of regret creak slowly open
Sealed by bulky days of contemplating
Exfoliating imaginary options;
Ceasing criteria to spoon-fed presumptions

How about garbage clad messages?
Cryptic, crawling six legged struggles
Beneath strain carrying reluctance

All the personal greed pools we hide in;
Glossed, shimmering legacy
Overflowed to become everyone's angst
Sputtered and spit;
Sand tied lashings judged, spotted, flashed and grabbed at
All the mocking fingers – so playful
Temptation;
I've always had trouble with the truth...

Monday's Synaxis

I can tell by your smile that you know what I mean
Carousel wings; Laser beams
Glide thru dreams;
It seems;
Evident, I love too many

Move, dropped from indigo outlets
Slipped, re-gripped, unzipped
Were you developed when Ed died?

Prison scheme
Milky chlorine
Scream when you cream
Swallow the shallow alternative routes of escape

Passive pup, bullwhip stuff
Turnout check, vacant neglect
A matted up sorry follicle descends to stapled tile

Extinguish with laughter;
Epoxy I'm after
Egotists aren't talking shit about anybody else but themselves...

Semen adhesion;
An HIV lesion
Chasing their dinner around the house with a Bengal potion

(I'd hate to bruise your trip, fired from the hip, it's infamous...)

A wish for a fish that backorders sheep
Alter bound; Across town
Hauled to the deep sleep

Unjust

Speaking to walls, crumbled to sand
In my crawl to devour turquoise lumps of dropped dust
Gravity's knuckles drag through patches of stale meteors
We toss them back and forth like clustered pink marbles

Microscopic withdrawal of cavern's chasms;
Cliffs too large to litter
Murderously impotent murmurs,
    Threats perform for ones un-wasted

Universal outings unplumbed in their soft moral petals
Masks of unjust;
Premeditated mistakes
Violently delicate strands of doubt creep and slither the motives
Purple and whimsy faced precognition

Bruised lantern jaws lean toward landscape land-filled lashings
Display carefully the landlord's unjust after their own edible debris

Fit, fat for a kingfish trash digger
Licking slowly and sucking up on the cavity eroded
Not too close, you may fall in...
Unjust;
Bury you useless

Bruised Crickets

Suddenly, sifting through soiled garments
The Whore was a bore, on her back,
Did she snore a fresh new sound?

Wrists are bound
A constant pound
Screams are drowned out by persistent lashing
Bitten tit
Bruised, swollen clit
Can't walk
Can't sit
Lying supine and breathing slowly

Beaten close to death   ,
Can't recall all of the rest
Mascara smeared
Acidic tears
Purple trails on motel pillows,
    She cleaned herself up

Life is tough
Lips are rough
"I've had enough"
She said on the way out, leaving

Dropped off the key
Not getting paid
That's no way, to get laid
Out the door
Out the hotel
The Whore she stands on the corner waiting;
Next . . .

The (rapist)

Face contorts
Clichéd bitten lip and rolled eyes
Look of struggle and reluctance to be conquered
Foggy rear view of headlights
Calloused blisters cover the silent scream
Muffled amplification of a victim;
A rag
Used and tearing at life's seam
Grease is not evident,
    For the trembling stranger is counting and seeing the bowling girls-

No more grey
No more sweat
The pain runs down her thigh and is complete
Soaked into the epidermis
Buried;
But convenient to recall…and deny.

Disregard

Autumn palominos,
   Forever in the doldrums
Winged, serpent lover,
   Doubtful of all revisions
Coniferous timber;
   The heart of our domicile

An owl's panorama stings homage to the view
Soulless matador's clitoris quest
I'm famished;
   Our cabin sleeps on the harbor
   And languidly travels on
Money market mixtures are primeval,
   But eloquent-
Auto mechanics ingredient pretzels blend retirement
   Income before college
Municipal deposit research say
   "The client's university must invest!"
The music store managers I know get good head in
   Golf pro shops everyday
Sad that landscape architect retailers are using
   Leather software now
And you can really go far on ceramic tires, you know...
Regardless of the steel-belted mark up rate
Rubber is merely digital oil cloth
Whiskey pastels are making a come-back
But who really buys used peach garden hoses anyway?

Disregard (cont)

Chemical inspectors floss with hi-grade carbide piano wire
   Twice a day on the Greek's scholarship
Acrobats require cellular sand just to break even these days
My rocking chair phone has a fever;
But the accountant's screwdriver is a bit weak
I'll add more larvae ...

For Christ sakes don't key the billboard,
   I'm getting dizzy
Burn the health department with small rocket engines though
Latex drapery is coronary unless you hibernate its
   Marina Window Kings
If the painters are captured,
   There will be cleaner hemispheres and grateful laser defects
At least the cavern, marathon fish will eat tonight
If anything else ...

Sincere

This mess seems much too intense
Wasn't it much easier when we were getting undressed?
Now you feel and say,
  Those things I don't want to hear
You're waiting for an echo and I give silence
(That's sincere)

One Escaped...

One escaped;
Out of the dungeon and up my arm
Screams from the forest,
Scrambled and scattered-
Atop the backs of squealing mice

Amphetamine dream
Lied awake,
    Tied in a corner alongside apologies
Bleak, tender blur;
Emptying cysts
Battered, tattered, mistaken myths
Retold while drowning

Yearn for yarn
Scraping off scoundrels
Blue background for a film of haze-

The guard yelled, "Stop!"
Half-stepped, then jumped
Into the open legged widow below
A two mile drop,
It stopped,
Short of harmony...

Airborne sweaty corroded
Waxed, tattooed and eroded
Lifted by whittled nipples;
    Sun shriveled and dry

One Escaped (cont)

Windless ripped patch;
Tends to bite tendons that match
The denim sleeved steeped grave-
I ditched the bitch...
The dormant, now broken snake
Bait for a brittle, bitten beginning
Pieced apart and sliding...

Picked and discarded
Lost and uncharted
I have but one left for the road...

One escaped
One was raped
By the hand of its own

That trembling face;
I struck it
With shatter comes blood
Hunched pleasantly over
Heave heavily into the Sinks of Sparkle

The green gush
A rush;
All too familiar

Pastel travel,
    A brown towel
Blue jeans and bare feet;
Asleep for three days straight ...

Lost Art

I consist of imperfection
Loose lipped conduct of ruptured has-beens
I'm wondering in bold faced social control

Failed, flailed, one and the same;
You're beaten down
Conceived to suffer; nurtured to inevitably die
How ironic is it that we are all well aware of this?

Open door shadows creep wide-eyed into us and then go astray...

Caterpillar vault shrivels to baritone mishaps-
Aquarium baptism, legacy tissue washed indefinitely
Clitoris mesh mesmerizing suede atmosphere

Sunflower, Sunflower
Sun shining gypsy
Beaded stringent insomnia;
    I am completely dubious
Handsome, hard-nosed defecation
Battered, retained and valiant

I cry awkward, cause I forgot how to . . .

Sex and Nature

Sex and nature
Undiluted jagged mischief
Seemingly black and white;
   Spliced together like an old film

Controlled excerpts, engraved in the brain
Taken outside and beaten
Conducted before the kids and the reporters and the audience
They were swearing and hurling debris
Not at them, but at me

No one doubted my glare, the demands I made clear
Mystique would release me from conforming to now exploding cheers
What was I alluding to?
Probably validity…
Consciously laced hypnotic holocaust

Anxiety-stricken shrill screams
Crawling, lime covered friends
Attend restrained distinction,
   Between shocking green ideals

Pathetic Princess Attempts

The girl next door has just gone mad, and I'm glad
Folks must have seen it coming, with the innocence up and running
Licking on shafts swollen; holing and poling
More than ever needed…

Back to front…from the beginning…

Try harder to impress me;
Tire me of your Pathetic Princess Attempts to prevent basic elemental
Intellectual instinctive dialect;
Rehearsed rhetoric;
Lesbian heretic;
Hands down (my pants?), it wins; grins
Subliminal and I'm not laughing…

Play on words,
Absurd and blurred, beyond bare-ass lashings
Goodwill is a store
A good will is one that is properly prepared
Don't Stare…

The casket is open and all is well
Your eyes swell
What the hell, one tear fell

In the bath is where he was found;
I don't think he drowned
Head held under, from evil hands I wonder;
    The porcelain above the ground
And the glass has to be full;
Bottle in front of me; another liquid lobotomy

I Dream

I dream of worlds that I perceive are out there
I dream of the world I hope is beyond my present comprehension
The dreams;
The dreams of youth and vigor
I dream and thus become it
This dream;
Dreams of travel, dysfunction, alienation
I'm in love with obstruction...
That grey matted ripple between fantasy and reality
That 'R' word I loathe;
I dream to view a shambles around me

Disheartening as seen by affluent strangers;
I would surely go mad in my solitude if I dissected life
    Any more than I do now

Apparent as just-fit stormy shores
Almost too cognizant of jagged let-downs
Sustain and wallow;
Cling to languid shellfish that will soon be the precursor
    Of my ailment

. . . I'm glad I saw you coming for the first time today;
You let me watch all the frustration, concentration and anticipation
    That kept you from being free
It just seems that everyone is on the rag today except for me . . .

Maybe through the entire gloomy visage, my smile is showing
Your skies are black and dormant;
My zephyrs are still coolly blowing

Leopard Propeller

Cement isn't harvested and you can't weld stone
Heat the pool while you're at it...
The President gets blown in the prop-plane
Grocery painting molesters are experienced pilots
Dig air conditioned trenches, too
The pipeline printing press is complete
Hey listen;
Whip this shit into a batter and serve chilled
Then cycle across the lake to the checker board bank teller
The child's piggy bank is in the sum of hand-woven rugs
Jogging by canoe is part of flight training
The winding road resort was just a retired school bus on blocks
But the annual orange acid fest breeds mobs
Bulletin maintenance;
One hundredth of an ounce
Alternative label;
Drink the license
Excess riot, dig?
Jewelry aircraft performance
Calm-Air-Winds-Tickets
Reserve boat silversmiths;
I can fly if need be man . . .

Simulated Serene Orbital Illusion

Beaks buried angst floating
Puncture sand nipple, ripple eroding
Grain of sane,
Speckled membrane

Epic proportions chipped, chiseled and made to be sprawling

Flaws carried
Viking rite pictured neutralized changing
Defending obscure;
Allowed exposed simulated serene orbital illusion

S. F. Canyon

My hills are burning
Tomorrow, I see the charred forest
Turned upside down and dipped in asphalt;
   The mountain tops
Death is black
Gray and soot
Glided by at sixty-five
Stripped of its green swirled world
Propellers sprinkle could not drown its spewing coils

World on fire
My little one -
Next Bardo passing from elder to birth

Veins throbbing spectacle onlooker
Cycle as us;
Brittle, dry, fragile, enduring, ending . . .
Just as us -
Mending and caring for until no longer able . . .

She Is You

She spins in bliss on the open floor
Leaving herself for a moment impure
Her mouth drafts a chorus of a window left ajar -
Careful not to unveil the moonlit tile
Illuminated;
The beam ricochets and finds the scar -
   A painless souvenir of a day not fond of . . .

Dizzy with fancy
Sculpting this fictional shape
Slightly tormenting the hopeful relief of tedious dismissal

She misses caring
Sometimes distracted solely on her stability

This insular region dislocated on tip-toes and fringes
Blowing years off dormant containers;
   Layers of tired hatred
Cloaked restriction of boundaries distorted by imposing eyes
Curving smoothness of notched riddles; Blunt direction

Pointed, told to leave
Rigid ignorance;
Drowning intellect;
My belief is her neglect -
   I feel so hopeless . . .

Forty Seven...

Forty – Seven close friends gathered around enduring tents
   In harnessed desert chasms
Wounds to realize
Scars released to prior influential, phony options

Obsessed to shake out discouraged risks;
   Exploded into bizarre creation

Trapped in the middle
Orange, droopy and thrusting
In between a pilgrimage of analysis;
   Corruption

Wrinkled Orchards

Saints swinging from cherry stem lines
A ratchet to the head,
   While sleeping in vines
Spring fling;
Abundant love
Hail of howls from the draw above

Drenched in sludge
Pouring flowers on my tongue;
   Spotted and streaming

Scratched on the redwood
Not graffiti to me
Sailor to the moon;
   Ripe hypocrisy
Wrinkled Orchards, Bruised Crickets
Infant ships drowned in murmurs
Carefully trapped and once again in love

Secret Knowledge

Secret knowledge;
What an attractive way to put it
Bizarre band of worshippers,
    Developed to martyrdom
Agitated, but knowingly inferior

Storm fatal rumblings;
    Clashing defiance
Immersed into infinite liberation
Concealed bliss bleeds barbaric cautious deism

Weary to isolate redemption and reality
Red wine and raw opium
Restoration;
Inserted and streaked kinetic duality
Gaining the attention of the master of never-ending struggle

Incubating calculated predictability
Repressed and festered;
    Rise above hazy compromise and undue pressure
The product of separate, arbitrary insecurity

You tell me...

You tell me I've had enough
Mash whiskey, in another paper cup

But to stop so abrupt,
    And travel the highway used less -
Would impede my onward voyage to the road of excess

Apple Orchard Marathons

Being chased by land owners with eloquent ideas
    On raising trepidation
The persona you protrude;
Subdued; Rude
Ripe, twisted and overdue
The more alcohol, the more I like you

Fixed your calamity
Fifteen year old boy with only one leg
A gimp with a peg
An ampu-teen?
(Was that mean?)

Crank call widows with collect calls from dead husbands
    Who died on coal barges-
Bad taste I know,
    But will you accept the charges?

A Bystander in a Box

How many times have we been through this?
I feel like a parrot;
    Going over and over the things that we said
Infested by a state of minuteness,
We frolic and stomp through faintly lit streets
Steel covered window fronts decorated with
    Multi-flavored murals
Emitting from the ground,
The funk of years and hours of constant mass transportation
An almost counter-culture of its own;
The subway scene

Taxis attempt to devour us in relentless recklessness
Screaming through the canyons of the city
This yellow peril;
    A species all its own
Overrunning the paved ways

Drudgery of existence
Equivalent of a mushroom in a darkened cave
My house is action packed boredom
Carry me through ailments;
    Bold-faced excuses
Blinking, jaded cultural downhill enthusiasm

A Bystander in a Box (cont)

Visit ancient ponderances and day old imagination
Modified dreams pieced together, and efforts so great
   To remember them upon reverie

Exotic stripper mesmerized by ginger bread limerick
Fanciful fuck-fest depository of caged boiling resilience
Shovel brooding governors into spacious loathing

Cadaver, Cadaver
A bystander in a box

Thru These Eyes

I view in silence from the third floor balcony
Parallel in elevation,
    Poles apart in life
Oblivious to all barriers;
Acknowledging only reality

Colors;
Icons;
The delicate reverberation of natural pristine beauty
Through my eyes,
    I enviously look on

The Termagant

The Termagant
Winsome, demanding
Placed on my knees,
    My cheeks slid up the thigh until it reached the hiatus
My nostrils flared,
    Fervent to enter
At first;
Uninviting and hesitant
Now ardent to continue
My tongue lashed out;
    The viscid sauce was emitting
I can taste it -
Watch it flow down the high-heeled limb
I spread it with my fingers;
It lingered; pulsated
No longer quiescent
She had quivered thrice and was close
(She told me)
My mouth numb and tepid,
    I proceeded on . . .

Waiting for the Pleasant

My full moon is dancing
Happily churning in its ascent;
   Spinning wearily

Perhaps the fragility of it all -
Its mere existence;
   Simply dwindles at our fingertips

Frothing, over friendly quirks and niches
More than social stitches
Vast arrays of stars and formality
Squeeze stiffly the vain bindings

Eat the dissolute earthstar
To no avail,
   A reckoning is served
A high rise splat is viewed from the hillside
The scene of the nomadic playground
Nylon domiciles on plastic plateaus
Shaggy green limbs and exposed toes

Now put into perspective;
   A universe without purpose
Indefinite cells and particles,
   Caressing gently in my index digit
A world all its own;
   Standing here, it all comes together
Completely overwhelming, unknown and complicated

The Impostor

From around the corner of its flourish,
    The children leapt out on The Impostor

I misinformed them all and veered them wrong -

They went off skipping and content with my pretension . . .

Forward Rolling Daisies

Slipped thru grids;
   Square matted burrows
Landscaped, slivering footsteps talk to crushed toes
Weary manicured obstinacy;
   Shrieking with wisdom

Absurd and delinquent
Killing a man about to commit suicide
Or
Proudly declaring your virginity,
   Only to get raped by your audience

Fragile cards bitten
Severed like new meat brought on by tolerance
This blue streak saw its descent
Tunnel forced to trip on its halt of Forward Rolling Daisies

Stranded Blink

Complicated as once I saw fit
Stones lined up to travel;
    Anchored rivals in cheeks pitted...

Collected scenes;
    Flirting with dysfunction
Broken confessions dance forward thru timeless deportation

Fallen girls I considered at a time
Bent whereabouts unknown
Unseen, earnest revalidations of one-act twists
Memories of me; them
Cluttered aspects of marvelous comfort and thorns

Uncoiling to a taut remembrance of a jaded letdown
Now;
    A precious memory

Birth and Death of Man

The universal merging of the leviathan phallus
   And the abysmal cavity
Thrusting forward;
   Plunging deeper into the seemingly insatiable chasm of time
The infinite orgy reaches its stellar climax -
   The Birth and Death of Man

As the temples pounded...

As the temples pounded and squealed with drugged-out sociability,
   Room sprang to life with sweat and conversation
Rubbed the ego
Massaged the libido
Torrid, non-descript

Emotional execution;
   Guiltless 'til the sour faces of winsomeness prevail
All the big retinas and surprised brows
   Following the insertion...
The swallowing;
The 80 proof shot,
   Taken now like candied fluid

Agitating, but still captivating
I have to view through marooned surprises
Unparalleled inability to conjure its drag and depression
Killing procrastination all together –
   - "fuck 'til tomorrow"
I'll put it off; Period.

Puncture regret with ice-pick thin despondence
Obstinate;
Socially ostracized;
   Approaching justification's back with honest indifference -

As the temples pounded... (cont)

Biting down on love of irrelevancy
Irrelevant;
    But worthy of acknowledgment

Through all the never;
    The never ending struggle
Through all the closed closet encompassing terms
We are left with "true" truth;
    The shit that is relevant

Secret things coupled with common fact
Nearly hundreds would have hinted toward dysfunction -

The same ones that bother the fuck out of your harmony,
    And rock your boat daily -
. . . Stupid shit like that . . .

Fanged Out

Fanged out at my incompetence
Scattered mind puzzles and boxed spot lit glory of
   Vibrant acclaim
Trapping coils;
   Entwined and becoming
Endearing tiny reflections,
   Ladle submissive profiles from the cauldron -
Mirror frightening claims;
   Square and unattractive
Wind chimes smash angrily against broken visions
Shattered progression;
   Burdened and absent of all originality
Stripped, unbalanced evolution

Depressed Buttons Grounded

Reach up and choke the disapproving, suffocated eyes
    That bred the fluttering monarch
I got flowers and days to color...
My anecdote beams and shafts of disheartened particles
    Soaring in glide
Atop my carousel; motionless

Spinning woven delicacies,
    And dust-pan corridors
Languid, tiny dots of vigor and retention;
Rich siege of reflection;
    Conquering blur and detection

Stenciled lashings and frequent symbols of pinwheels
Pissed on my new juice;
    A soiled suit
A parade of half-squinted eyes -
Stopped short of contact;
    Brushed lightly

For a moment,
    Disrupted and upset
Depressed buttons grounded;
For one second,
    Fleeting and illuminated;
They were mine . . .

The Hunter

A kestrel soars above the draw
Atop the stallion he waits;
    The Hunter
Dismount and align it with your target;
    The begetting forest silhouette

The projectile flies
Life is pierced;
    Red snow

The Hunter crouches over the earth mother's child
Still breathing;
    Gasping for life
Out of mercy or respect
A gunshot rings;
    Thru the canyon floor and off to heaven -
The world dims; life ends

The Hunter tramps through the virgin white chasm
Dragging behind him,
    What nature left vulnerable and unprotected

The once brown mass of death is white and frozen now;
    Eyes azure and cold
Frustrated sun;
    Breathes out clouds of discomfort to its aborted child
Life is grey . . .

Glass Rats

Glass rats hemstitch obscurely,
　　Those quinine blankets of dust
Drowned salmon talisman with oratory syndrome;
　　Down with tweed slacks and fat hatchbacks

They drive to the parliament orgy held at the semantic pond
Sun and Sky;
　　Consumed right from the bottle
Mince pie and bourbon runs bowels red.

Dancing on the Devil's Tongue

No problem pull- ups on mustache riding harlots
Plant shit up your ass;
        Separate inside cunt journeys ended
At a moment's exit,
        I'd turn into a wreck

Two lovers merge to exit the overpass
        Onto below humming cars
Sun worshipping; bronzed and glowing
Brown Buddha's covered with oils and jewels
Bull whip hair-snapping and
        Stinging the wind passing deity
Sweaty neglected ones;
        Exclaiming rear end tremor

Dancing on the Devil's Tongue
Pointed in two and poisoned;
        Some things are much more appreciated than smothered
Days of rejoice
Empowering, embracing smiles
Captivating, languid travel;
        Those special ideals
Yield to frail eyes behind thick blankets concealing
        Frigid obscenity . . .

Dancing on the Devil's Tongue (cont)

Oscillating fans a blowing;
  All the shit I be knowing
Dust accumulating and collecting in the corner of my eye
What a valid reason to cry;
  But to die ...
I guess I'll have to find one better than that

Vice on heart;
  Good inward inflection
Believe abound voices
Farewell to unaware, naked undertones
Planted shadows imprisoned to wonder

Disciple like a bird;
  Poisoned and creepy
Heart complains aloud;
Terrible,
Proud,
Worried climbing.

Mental Riot

Mental riot
Waves of feeling
Cerebral storm

Electric
Veins amplified
Arteries aesthetic

Intense
Majestic
Overwhelming

Pulsate/Throb
Precipitate
Sweat

Crawling,
Formless organism

Complete evolution;
Metamorphosis

Death
Nothingness
Rebirth

Narrow Splinters

What can I say of my view?
Not often enough,
    I'm up here
Poured into this canyon
Rolling up and down these Narrow Splinters

The sun peers its curious head over lofty summits
Occasionally spilling angled shadows into the draw
Embracing the evening's dying -
Its last stupor before the day's birth
A solemn moment;
    A blinding course

Trailing silently
Humming along its intruding path
It treads on;
    Through the divide and following

Tormented messengers speak to the welcome morning
Timid little burrows;
    Hidden thorns pierce uninviting dogma

Binding plunge of corralled willows
Nestled in the Tanager;
    Encased in gated envy
I downshift,
    So as not to disturb . . .

Now it's Confirmed

It always appeared as a crevice
Extinguish my premise;
    My demise

Featured in sneering deserts
Flirted pygmy dignity dildos smothered incumbent
A burden to didactic rhetoric;
    Indeed conspicuous

Brash side-show verdicts
Elevated elephants tempted by paprika's cyanide enthusiasm

Nobody kept jigsaws entangled
Deejay altered brilliance,
    But was too cynical-idealist
(Hung over the mantle)

Now it's confirmed…

Killing my Bending Neglect

Almost as if pacified;
   Affluent Angel
This little whip
Lost in a world I know so well
Petite petal dancer

Breaking bladed waves, I turn
Lashed back;
   Pushed forward and assaulted
Eager pillar people;
   Gargoyle buttress soaring atop serenade

Crash is sailing
I think I hear her
Piss is passing me by; as is curing foam
Clever was never used before lever;
   It was smart to pull at that time

Derived by bruising;
   Tree top to tree top
Shipping baby-girl
Greased, swinging reason -
What complicates nudity?
Compared to what ignites thru you

Killing my Bending Neglect (cont)

Fat trouser marks;
    Open car windows
Broken heels on borrowed shoes

Killing my bending neglect;
Loose spiral inverted nipple
Comatose
Sucking on the cork from the night before
Oscillating eyelids;
    Cross-surfing on shackled seas
Still;
    Test tube children and four legged stifling

When the dancing is done,
    I run to you
You say you understand
I love you
I need you
I don't want you
I want someone who doesn't need me;
That's what I want
That's what I need

I Cancun

Titles crack with pressed up bodies;
   Slamming bones and flesh
Slippery floors and sweaty walls
Nails sharp and flailing
Bitten neck and punctured cheeks;
Blood saliva,
   Smoldering breath
Liquor-fuck;
   Friendly ending courtship
What nice, nameless, faceless girls...
Exciting, exiting eyes;
   Wondering smiles
Thank you;
   Gone; next

Syntax-subtle bombing
Melodramatic surprises
Like a quiet bulb,
   I swallowed it whole
Wired, whisper coming;
   Hit head on
Neon green chassis
Suspended on the hook line
Criminal grin;
   Con (cealed) smile

Recline and arise sweaty
On grey earth,
   Under black running showers

We boarded the plane and smiled . . .

Tap Dance Mitigation

Hit the brakes -
Stop the world -
I want to get off

What will I wear to my execution?
White winged waves;
    I'm stressed

Throw out the life line
You wrap it around your throat
I'm stripping my gears
Full of shit;
    You choke on it

The last time I saw him,
    He was in a coffin
Empty and deflated

Tripping over the holy man
Speed bumps in the street
Hap-hazard creeps;
    Spoon under cheeks

Collect your tears;
    You feed it to me
Open;
I taste your fears
Swallow slowly;
    Me

A Strain to Remember

As the lemmings continue toward the sea
We are rushing toward temptation as vibrant juices
    Sting our ever interfering tranquility
We hoard and coerce 'til mischief escapes scream
We rifle through excuses and glossy colored depictions
    Of faces that are now dead

In time,
People will view pictures of me the same way
You remember;
    For a minute
There are living things to do
Tonight,
    I don't want to sleep...

What is passionate to you?
And when does that passion become so much of a burden
    That it is deemed futile to carry onto what is believed
    To be un-nerving?
Sacred in your life...
Breeding differences and abhorrence

Oceans of dreams, revelations and given knowledge
Learned, absorbed and forgotten -
Inevitably alive for instances of gratification
Adorned,
    But misled justification

A Strain to Remember (cont)

True;
    Absurd to me
The trifling vibes that disturb me -
But true that they do

Forgiven innocence to the eyes you can't hide behind;
    They never lie
Mouth, heart, head often misleads
Eyes tell too much;
    Often enough

Glance to the floor for answers that never appear;
    Questions never made clear

Looking away from the truth;
    Looking away from you
Strange how we just know . . .
Those things so significant and special,
    Now a strain to remember.

Dancing Through the Bone Yard

Dancing thru the bone yard with open mouthed lashings
Licking temptation's salted fiber
Inciting impure tyranny and quarantined kindness

Almost deliberate in movement -
Leisurely striding distraughtly towards elements of
   Higher education

My crest fallen monologue;
   Purple sermon monger

Dramatize this isolation with closed curtain triumph;
   I can't wait to prevail . . .

Universal Cry

The Earth is scared;
    It trembles
We feed it contamination;
    Fill her belly with our debris
We drown her in fluids;
    Our mistakes and excess unwanted
Invisible to us;
    Oblivious to the problem

Dismember her skin
Cut her hair
Shear her limbs to assemble homes for us,
    While exiling her children from theirs

The Earth is angry
It's no wonder,
    Not often enough
That she shakes the shit out of us
As if to say,
    "What the fuck are you doing?"

Our Earth speaks; listen
It bleeds genocide;
    Swallows and absorbs all
It screams a universal cry for help
Like all others;
    We ignore it

It means Nothing

Don't jingle your keys in my face,
   I'll replace the linoleum myself
Change purse is empty though;
Take that fucking flag down
Your cat is frightening me;
Genital warts would be cursed -
Guess what I found in my sock?
Use a thumb tack...
If the honey can't reach it,
   Let it seep through
Did I mention that it's freezing?
The picture is crooked,
   So drive over my apprentice
Paper cups always make me smile;
Inhale the rayon...
Did someone leave the gas on?
The pine needles are hurting my ass, that's why!
Oh, please!
Take off that ridiculous sweater . . .

Veins Like Splinters

Riding on rivers, Veins like Splinters
Banshee screaming, tight-rope walking
Bound, gagged, confused;
    I'm watching you

I'm gonna crawl around
Won't you join me?
We could be so good together,
    Entwine yourself in me
Let's get tangled forever

Like flies
Spiders and the green wall-climbers
My pets, don't kill them;
    Flourishing and breeding

No longer gripping onto those possessions I wanted
Empty goals,
    Given into conformity flaunted
Fuck the stare; their glare
Mine is also strong

Peel it back
Exposed to show its, trickling, violet I know it
I told them to wait
They couldn't, they didn't -
I showed them my crumbling, clenching fist;
    Ending and molding

I'm alive but it's ending
There's too much water in here and
    The closer you get;
I need you now . . .

Brow wrinkles
You're getting blurry
Extend your hand;
    All the lines, they lead to me
Aware now and bewildered how,
    I did not notice before

Veins (cont)

Conscious is a constant scene
No longer green –
It's rusting, corroded and pissing off my world

That's all
You can kill the fucking children;
    You don't let them think for themselves at all
They're garden crops
Educated with grammar and theorem;
    Dead to sculpture and song

II.
She's my girlfriend, but don't tell her that
To her, she is only 'my girl'

Glass jars of hope,
    Lined up and shattered
I attack the impulses
Emotionless, twisted masks of anguish
Countless faces;
    Simulated surreal copulation

Behind the Tinsel border,
    My love left town
Abrupt, tenacious, wretched finger tips

Veins (cont)

Sewn casually;
    Bound to celebration by leg iron agony

Subtle groans
I'm in love with a badger –
Grey-haired sun
Beaded, flailing ignorance
Cherry cut,
    Marked obvious similarity

Suspicious substance
Rubbed coincidently on sedate, sheathed petals
Wondering un-earthy, thorny, oriented laughter
As if it was nude;
    Danced nude and running
Trickled down
Dangling on the toenail of horrific bedlam;
    A particular breech to your splintered friends
Exposed serene -
    You're cluster fucked . . .

Below they gathered;
    Apparent and displayed
Limbs spilling out onto liberated rigidity
United, (still pompous)
Rendered dramatic discussions . . .
Among thieves, actors and closed eyelids;
    Embodied, enticing, charmed numbing -

Veins (cont)

III.
Choked as it attempts to slither out to lost tension
Trail of jewels dropped here; there
Mocking pebbles frustrated spirit riddles,
    And sleazy abandoned darkness
Pushing in emptiness;
    Settled and un-nerving
The cocoon empowered sleepy monotony spewing forward
    To crumbling deprivation –

The thin membrane deviance,
    Sucking thru the straws of Middle America
Be the Christ you want to be –
Now is the elegance of your change and suffering

IV.
Temples pounding (just the left one)
Riot festivals altering friendships
Youth madness attorneys' erotic logical conclusions -
Impact matches,
Lit and burning;
    Between toes of admiration
Astoundingly trying to choke the masses
Climbing on young, east coast girls . . .

Furtive, anxious tongues
Touching parts meant to disgust

Veins (cont)

Panting about ranting -
    Eyes widen as she gyrated her minor theme
Legend would have it,
    Speckled in freckles
Laughter and discarded clothing

V.
Hollywood remains one of the few,
    Pseudo-gold street pavement hue
Sensitive, nocturnal, overwhelming
Trampling commotion;
    Luke-warm champagne
Subconscious ovation,
    Littered on the brain
South American drunkenness
Sentenced to depression
Antagonistic suppression
At a time when madmen would chase blind church
    Whores around our twisted universe
When fire penetrated drama,
    And wounded pumping solemnity

Intriguing as once I saw fit
Everything is not peaceful,
    Beautiful and worldly -
As I first saw it . . .

Veins (cont)

VI.
Gorgeous disaster; simple death
Too simple?
A flawless, intimate tribe

Incision cut
Arteries blurry
Surgery stewardess drank when no one taunted
   Antigone's human pyramid
She refused to laugh
Refused to column and balance
Hysteria continued ash-storms;
   Grabbed, fondled baited beginning

Suck a reincarnation
A hallucination of my shouting crotch
"Find a way to face-fuck your friends"
Showering years wailing;
   New Year's funky, pagan monkey
Demon priests looming on captured conscious
   Sexual tension –
Mysterious, brown and original
One critical and contrite ivy covered wall of complete control;
   Dramatic and extreme

Veins (cont)

VII.
Sum up the perpetrating bum
Never needing to cum
He's clouded his brain with cheap wine
    And tends to be glum

Pressure booking
Pouring public schlock
Media photos
Impotent politics;
    Possibly pricks
Blatant boutiques, 'ass buddies'
Weeks prior had padded their daily escape –

Liberate a sink
You drop a little lower
Inept to intercept;
    A reaching to scream

VIII.
Underground attention,
    Laced with frustration
Opinion of feedback suppression
Your crack addict comments
Rapt reasoning enough to worry even the most
    Creative of trolls

Veins (cont)

Probably withdrawn things;
I mean the beautiful things –
   That both bothers and disturbs me

IX.
Even as, such as now
I look back smiling on photos and entries of trips
   That I can't recall to a point of vividness
Even starkness;
Fragile memories cut and glued
Collage of disconnected crossing out and rewriting
   That satisfies my self reflect
As to viewing an unfamiliar work of 'shit art'
That is preposterous;
That is my life . . .

Of Mammoth Glossy Moments

Of mammoth glossy moments
Sinister unparalleled sarcasms
Impending balladry,
Prophetic echoes;
    Tremor biting Bohemian starvation

At last
Calm years languish
Smoky, narrow self-critical hatred;
    Peck out discussion rather projected
Run down but moodier than before

Its Digesting Ramble

Outrage came,
    And we gripped its digesting ramble
Under the same breath
More obvious diadems would softly sift
    Above the thatched view below us

Secure behaving
Discussing; paraphrasing
Fittingly unable to avoid the axe in your back;
    Impaled with gold, frustrated incapability
Instrumental to fantasy;
    Rapid pivotal sufferer
Define deep-settled trauma
Manifested, overturned agenda
Such a volatile ego;
    Ill, but dealing with encounter

Plugged by peers
Shocked thru rock
Crowd would shout its plausible crisis
-What now deems to be immediate accompaniment-?
A tremendous rush,
Contrary to design;
    Instigated accidental ancestry

Its Digesting Ramble (cont)

And so it be;
Spontaneity
Accelerated descendant;
    Commitment to struggle
Thrust into and compel
Collapse;
    Edge of an overdose
Swim to aspects
Speculate stabbing pity
So close;
    Madness just made it worse

I turn over;
    Play possum
Coughing up white chalk meant I had enough.

Sublime

A place to burrow
A place to hide
Away from streets and phones;
  Open and outside

A room
An escape
A serene place to retreat
To gather thoughts and reason
Ones to absorb;
  Ones to delete

Picking out memories,
  From baskets of youth
Green and vivid;
  Shrouded with truth
Worlds of lasting beauty
  And timeless grace
Held broken;
By a wrinkling, tired old face
One that frowns,
  After often seldom smiles
The one that loses sight of what it is all about;
  After awhile

Sublime (cont)

Untwined and separate,
    From the lessons I've learned
On the foot of their disapproval
I drop this excess baggage;
    Of my less concern

So I tread on,
    In search of this place
To view and quietly sit -
A special sanctuary;
    Away from life's everyday bullshit
I will find this place
It will be mine;
    Sublime

Electric Telepathy

Why am I sinking?
The tile is cracked
   And I'm entering the sweet,
   Golden incline
Textured, flat exuberant fiber;
   The shit of millions
Electric telepathy
Pierces acute with needle thin reason
"you die motherfucker"
   shovel this-
   pick up this-
   eat me...
Dirty slit eyeball gave us ink
He bit it;
   Where did it go?

Refrain your tremble
   And lie supine
Tack in your back;
   She put it there
I'll race you
I'm laughing;
   You got no piece of me
Untwist and decline in it

Six Feet Blunder

Embalming my fortune
Disappearing into 'come again'

Payment for a plot
Paying for my future rest spot

They withhold my finance for days of
    Leisure and old age
Knowing I'll never live to get it

Pompous Prophet

Sculpted by the wind
Breathe deep;
    New view with each blink
By morning's rising it will be a memory

Pyramids placed intricately atop my forefinger
Camel's back;
Outstretched crest tucked
    And pressed against the black sky
Desert eyelids;
    Closed tantrum castles

These eroded storming moments
Cleverly blinding sand stories of the escaping ones...

Led tranquility;
Sifting beyond this vast empty contrast
Azure and tan
Met in conjunction
    At the horizons midst of anguish and arid consciousness

I wish to be lost in the desert
Under my nails and skin;
    Caked and embedded in my turban of inebriety
I am my own pharaoh . . .

Addicted to the Prince

Addicted to the Prince,
  Scuffle for the rift
Lizard biting fish
Tease for love, prejudice, suspicion
Once I loved;
  I don't know if I ever will again

Succubus,
  Take me in my sleep
Succubus,
  Climb with me

I don't know what to think anymore;
Everything is so odd...

Clothes hanger feticide
Malted glucose in a jar
Reservoir unicorns
  And taciturn dwellers unite

Reluctant to follow;
  Second wagon route
Primatene to lead
Their philosophy is shit;
  Squeeze and ooze out my hand
A hefty dose for their own breakdown

Tremble

I can see pictures of the faintest of things
In suffering circles;
Our compassion is drawn
With grey mist and roaring clarity,
    Drugged Cannons Whisper

Dancing reapers of chaos in misplaced boxes
Pressing pianos up mole hills
The conceit,
As it hardens,
Is dead

Drop enrichment bombs on our heads
Demand the frantic awakening;
    The depth and smell of secular love
Uncertain of predictions that make me a prince
    Of underground castles of doubt

Even my elbows are soiled
Up to my neck; I dove in
The routes were mine
Their character planted firmly in silence
Quietly naïve;
    Frantic and afraid

Acid Reign

Gray Jesus
Open up your unassuming sanguine skies
Inundate us;
    Precipitate our sullen lives

Clandestine sun
Embrace the wind with your ominous arms
Lacerate the clouds
Dismal;
Macabre;
Mundane;
Soil us with your generous offering;
    It's drowning, flowing abundance . . .

Consecrate

Can't the geese see they're falling?
Tapping the fragile needle in and out of consciousness
Biting down upon a frown, fetal response
Attacked by sheaths of fallen feathers;
    I melt into trickled disappointment

Ordered to blend into the ice of toes on
    Chauffeured monks led to their pact
Poured bourbon and lit matches
Square upholstery emitting no protest,
    But sparking anguish

Flaming silence
Unaware he was being rocked to sleep
Once again,
    Reveled in the yellow ashes

Separated, placed on foreheads of disfigured scribes
Feed charred notes of unusual pleasing
"think nervous green piercings"
Kind hands rewind retracting thorns
Infected danger tissues and hangnails;
    Outgrown and grasping at matador's opus

Soiled cosmic orchard;
    Ruptured by imperfect chasing
The slow sinking of the lamb

Explode

Don't hide;
Their time will come
The grime will make me dizzy...
If all aspects arise to wonder,
    If all things conjure
At war with defiance;
Alliance,
    Of trite spanning days
Colors of hue;
Too bright to know their names

Of basic travel
Planned out and paid to lose
Slipping without friction;
    Gone to seek the truth
All that talk of retention,
    And secret things I've learned
Forgotten too simply;
Easily pressed to admire

Now is that neat tab to puncture
Yellow dripping wireless cavity;
    Crawls languidly through narrow statements
Incense moth feels the way of the circular strain
Half-striped crescent dictating the degree of its own pain
Hung neatly
    And ready to explode

Jagged

Sheltered skull in my marsupium
Carrot flag shank pierces flagellant caribou
North Pole decisions are made with linear pitch
Edacious piranhas are anorexic while misfortunate abundance
    Conceals treasures of pungency

This swarm of antics;
    Dusted, frothing lava
Jaw's vivisection splits the legacy with splintering ashes of nectar
Burnt with conceptual kindling;
Mindless limp-dick star plow ungainly kills wild caramel smiles
Iron whore jesters, naked in fields of mildew...

While damp with faint memories of oil kisses and caressing yellow –
Interpreting my vacuous offering;
    My eyes glaze over
Give me a wing to hide behind

Serrated and faded
Dulling and self-inducing
Sanctioned by reluctant curiosity,
    Its path becomes milky and narrow
My witness is no longer silent and alone;
I don't miss a detail
Continual spiral feelings;
    I can no longer distinguish my own skin from touch

Jagged (cont)

My colors gel and I know I've reached it-
As close as I can get
I'm there . . .

My approach is fraudulent,
    Though my intentions are sincere
I'm torn;
I want to be fat and worthless

My ideals and values are at war
I cannot choose a side
I collaborate, but I'm confused
I don't want to choose...
Yet, the two cannot fuse...
I lose . . .

High Pitched Tornado

Since its inhibitions flourished-
Confined water,
    Not the same blue as from above
Ebbed grey matted ripple
At quiet war with collaboration;
Dead to the middle

The crown that claims crests,
    Spawn out to each other
Inching forever forward to dwindle
One tract collides...
It doesn't have to be that way

Rub gently the smooth;
Stroke the fluttering wings and,
Stir up waves of heat and,
One tiny moth frantically beats its limbs into a frenzy and,
At the touch of a button we feel the torment and,
Now the high pitched tornado whispers and,
At last,
    Peaceful, gentleness is piped into us...
Where is the criticism and utter despise?

Perils of Fidelity

Don't be hesitant to absorb what will eminently prevail
Choice in the matter amounts to quality
Many days are numbered such after thoughtless repetition
Condensed and concentrated core moments and events;
Times of maze and confusion are best;
    Lost and fading
Broken in half and living self-contained

What's it all about?
This...
These nights and secrets;
    Torn, silent and breathless

Two strangers spinning wearily
Dizzily faint with no destination
How can I explain?
I live for this;
    These minor occurrences
Regarded as little, fleeting shit to some

Lying is often mesmerizing
Still;
Falling;
Inside, everything has stopped functioning properly

Perils of Fidelity (cont)

Chin tucked into your shoulder
Squeezing my torso tightly;
   Stopping just short of discomfort
Under fate and spell;
   Assaulted by no one
It was you
I studied the visage;
   I could trace it with my eyes closed
My explanation made sense-

It means nothing more than what it is;
It symbolizes fear and 'why?'
Who cares?
It's here and very attractive
Ceasing it could be done,
   But why?
This is absolutely what it is all about
The direction we are going...
What we will remember...
What we can't forget...
Not the game or show,
   But for real;
Now---

Five Tiered Fetish

Stomping on a paper crown;
  The empathy that keeps me down
Stifling sickness and weakness are flogging me
Happy hornets stinging tattoos on my skin;
Got a jam-spread Scorpio honey-dripper;
The jam-packed smack lover

Over crowded plastic grins-
Tired, tiny fingers squeeze out the view
Shackled eyes,
  They lash at you
Vast tenacious selected symptoms are climbing me;

Aboard contentment
Affecting radiance
Atomic sleeper just a limp-dick length away from obscurity;
  Relative, punctured prosperity
Circling like a vulture,
Looking down on me-
Five Tiered Fetish;
  My depravity

Stood in the Morning

Those little fuckers are already here...
As usual;
The norm;
Inevitable-

Black and grey with red horns and curved feet
Quads tight and squirming
All better to chase me with;
I usually don't run
Stroked so smoothly,
    I instantly surrender-

With brows raised,
    They look on smiling with closed, tight mouths
I stare back as if to silently, passively resist...
They laugh wildly
They know;
They got me beat
They know it and I believe it.

Tied to a stake
Buried indefinitely in hard-packed soul;
    Left with minimal tether
I make it on the minimal;
    Essentials

Stood in the Morning (cont)

I shit in the same place I lay
A lot of time,
    Right in the middle of it
I tire quickly and immobile I remain-

Panting and sweating
The control has chaffed my neck and left me for disposal
Oh, tomorrow I'll revive...
Dizzy, weak and discouraged;
    I'll whisk and flail
Furtive as a hummingbird's wings flutter,
    I'll pull and tug to break restraint
I know it's futile;
I have known this ...

Upon contemplation I start digging;
Deep;
Deeper;
Legs, hips, torso-
I'm in;
Buried
In the hole...

It is that time again-
They have returned...

Stood in the Morning (cont)

Fill my bowl?
Give more movement?
Cut this fucking rope!
I have tried...

Bitten and ravaged at the cord sinew
I'm not rewarded, I'm beaten
Flagellated and reminded of just what I am...
There is no custody here—

I'm tied to myself;
I turn to see the two-headed monster
The rope is like twine;
    Breakable by the hands of a small child

This is my dragon;
If he is not there, facing me in the morning;
Brows furrowed with anxiety-
I go look for him
I always find him-
He's not far-
He is never far away from me.

Strenuous Haphazard Tumors

You ignore the things I say,
    The things I slur
Can't accept;
Make a mark, make a stir
At least you react in some way-

Live ignorant; shallow
Dive into it but watch your head;
    Lead, and sink in deeper
I couldn't move without bumping into a wall
Surrounded by doubt,
    I have got to move on...

You stamp your feet;
    Your eyes say otherwise
You turn to me as if to say different-
I stand; staring
That's scary...

Episcopal planetary faith-healer
Kayak is caught in traffic on frail collarbones
Pigeon toed oligarchy;
    Non-graduate existential brash visionary-

Strenuous Haphazard Tumors (cont)

That is the one I love...
For once; projected
A noble nobody;
Inhibition's chasms open Strenuous Haphazard Tumors –
The ones of inertia and old age
Malaise delinquent malaria clasp into Berlin
    And choke the memories of normal tidings...

I'm tearing at crucial points of my scream;
I can see the pale green contrasting.
Knowing all too well, it will soon sink if left to drift...
Burn the nervous vessel;
    Just to swim back to the shore

11:32 p.m.

Emperor's daily daffodil
Magellan would be proud to primp taciturn seeds;
  A commodore's Tachina fly
Hydrophobic respell eluded prowler's waxy unraveling of
  Prevalent mishap edacity-

Soaring, colorific fascist farmers
Creep aphetic noise to beam the somatic carte blanche
Wispy wise, I realize;
  Dope sick on Pig's invasion
Short-sighted trifling; repeated garble
Finnish investment pestilent wretch!
Highly recommend reclamation on blindfolded envy...

Unfold, taut dauntless messiah;
  Napoleonic reactive childhood

12:41 a.m.

Unaware of the passing hour . . .

And then it happened ...

Smiling like a bending highway;
   It happened...

Tears they flow
Tears they stain
If left alone, they go away

When it all comes together, we smile
And even in moments so dismal and desolate,
   After awhile,
   We smile-

So much
So hard;
   Too young
Who hasn't gazed into deep vision?
Content to amend previous affirming...
Everywhere is polluted with worthless ideals;
   Moral illusions
Treated as chained servants

Pride;
Truth entwined havoc
Good speech indoctrinated puncture-
Needle mark scars;
   Love who you are

And then it happened ... (cont)

Renounce ugly sentiment with jovial resentment;
It's secreted thinking...

Scare yourself;
    Exalt cowardly concern for shallow equality
Worship warships...

I retire my eyes and aim my mind to favorable implanting.

Limitless;

Dark;

Unaffected and unbiased . . .

A sun that only shines on me;
    Everyday
No clouds, except for the one I'm on
Pointing and laughing;
Flocking with birds I ruffle fig leaves;
    Ascend and scatter
Call to conjure
A ring of fragility
We dove through endearing portals;
    Content with having prudence of everyone-

And then it happened ... (cont)

For once;
Frantic beast tip-toes to Boreas
Hiding in thickets;
Bending to prance on fallen vigilance
Given in to placid indulgence;
    If for once, it would forgive...

Nourishing little white words make
    Forgetful concern for innocence
Sweet moon child's notion to sex lion's secret, sacred transformation...

Shapes to shift
Stones to skip
Hips; bones crushing into dust
Rainbow freedom; dancing sky
Forbidden floors; intrinsic eye

Individual filth;
Impurity equates to wading in tubs of luke-warm triumph
Agitating, endearing neglect;
    Spilled over abundance

Insights to contrived weakness in high times;
    When the tides all flood into one
Bundled into blankets and blank faces;
    I wonder indifferent
I stray into what I become.

Thursday Afternoon

Explosion to faithfulness
Hexed;
    Undressed
Sun swarmed,
    Carpet warm
Attacking through open windows

Untwined to tangle
Limbs; arched bodies
Stabbed, pierced repeatedly—

Raised brows
Locked arms at the elbows

Sweaty and smug,
    Burns from the rug
On her back and on the knees of the one above ...

Blindfolded Napalm Flashes

In one enormous inhale,
   All numbness is sucked in
Squint to absorb;
Faded out to the stillness...

Of all the stones thrown;
Of all the threats I've construed-
I am still confused
Frantic;
But of what?
Maybe that is it.
I don't know what I'm afraid of and that
   Scares me to death

Astonishing fetishes sculpted through many favorable criticisms
Positioned at short, howling downed domesticity-
It is not traditional imaging;
   Maimed and twisted
Elaborate on what is seemingly maturing
Haunting, powerful indications;
These conjuring rehearsed ugly denials...

So long to complexities
So long to lines ...

Blindfolded Napalm Flashes (cont)

Incongruities and exhausting measures;
Obscured dismal fields blooming cool lava-flow
    Follow spinal renderings-
Flush with drawn rarity;
The spirits are laughing as you pursue the ancient
    Long revered shine on shadows-
Sun burn never felt like this;
Sun's embrace;
    A child's kiss

Isolation reaps echo;
    Transcribe sustained versatility
Automatic anything was intimate to technique...
Melodic flowers thrown; strategic wondering
Macabre, subconscious conjuring-
Bent and brutal functions behaving inadvertently...

Authoritarian;
    Blindfolded Napalm Flashes
Not surprised to sleep through permissive enthusiasms...

Rotten Cherry

Decrepit fetus,
    Unless crest riders break
Metralgia sets in;
Bristles soaked;
    Less abrasive to the exiting flesh
Shaved twill;
    Absorb the creeping flow
The thick fluid we're covered in at birth
And later;
Our cocks, tongues and fingers

Taste like tin;
    Concealing disease
A vehicle of death,
    Tearing at youth.

Drank in homage
Idol winery-

Symbolic of pain and monthly anguish;
    Poor girl...

Consequently Forgettable

All stings confronted, for the first time
Planetary greatness and witness stomped calling
Achieved deviance;
Molested with time-

Death of you benefits fantasy
Disliked retrospect hate things;
    Learned mistakes sustained creativity
Aware of superficial jaded advantage...

Frugal feud happens as beauty is battered
Crying previously; reaching defiance

Things pretty don't scar as much as ugly.
Weird is much more slicing-
Scared to powerfully reflect to abandon incoherence...

Hate, spoon-fed by a pretentious over-zealous trite configuration

Alley coyotes crooning all my sisters and brother
I don't know; you do know
Realize all the secrets of life, beauty and constant dying-
Fickle corners bend;
    Concealing wombs that only majesties possess

Consequently Forgettable (cont)

I think a lot about funerals and fingers;
Grabbing and clawing at senseless mercy and later;
    We will all be absorbed

Pillar plunger pathetic entrance;
    Let in to decide for themselves

As I tip the vat, my eyes widen to an all-time high
Brooding hazel wondering;
    Perpendicular horizon jagged emptiness
Sour tongues now fear entering...

Warriors?
I want peace;
Flowers, wind, tomorrow...
Give my afraid flavors contact;
    We dance to forget

Scamper to a plateau, and then look back in need
Squinted to golden threads-
Mountain lion wrath enveloped insanity...
Balcony possessed tan hip shake; descending footage
Distorted tinkering crashing down upon bland neon masses...

Consequently Forgettable (cont)

Sloped wretched gripping the finger grooved fungus-
Consumed concerned killer;
High cheek boned, handsome face much admired...

It is fine to be in character
But to a time you have to have an edge;
    Something to cut the pretension
Fear not...
Chin on my shoulder;
Breathe deep and casual

If you're waiting for bonfire; appease prejudice
Run to neck-tie law makers
Walk in on adultery (I'm one up on you...)

Poncho tight trousers hurt;
All perspectives and views are now relevant...

"...as time goes running off with our dreams,
    stolen hopes flash across vacant screens...
    pleasantly it seems;
    We are never more scared of life as we are now..."

Piercing Obstinacies and Innocence

As drops filtered thru my hand,
   I saw the forming
A pyramid of the fallen;

Hanging on to gravity,
   The last particle suspends acutely
Piercing Obstinacies and Innocence
Seduces my sky and stands broken-
Fragile me;
   I slowly attempt to preserve what's left to save
I love the clenching...

The sand patterns and desert quilts
Someone is wearing where I'd like to be-

Porpoise is kicking the camel's back;
   Rolling semen in my hand

Sprinkled granules wasted and weaved into;
   With the others

Ground dust;
   Tumbling bond will forever vivify individuality.

Liquid Perspective

Being wasted is a naiveté;
  A perfect veil for reality
My sober eyes realize what is fucked up
I obtain and put on those bourbon bifocals;
  Now I know what's up...

Vodka mesh;
  The best I get
I don't need too much to remember,
  I need a lot to forget

Pour me another,
  My brother
Chairs pulled up;
  Fill 'er up
My cup-
Torn up;
  But it's still not enough...

Altered

Rub its tail, it will react
Crystal chimney;
    Descend the black lizard
Down to the bottom;
Target analysis is hospital flesh
Too deep to claw its way back up...

Poison incision to carve the cure
The great totem looks great in its numbness-

No longer damp;
I lie limp
Swimming in my anesthetic-

I feel no pain
Diseased;
Reinforced;
Credible

I don't feel the enveloping darkness but I know its there...

Sachem of my own Scheme

Sachem of my own scheme and nomadic descent
Tribal whipping toboggan
Phallic turban unemployed; as always

Did you enjoy the binge?
Or the retreat of meager requests on his virtuosity?

Improper mastery of simplistic ordinances explode in
    Uninviting ears of disposal
Temporary listener's veracity
Pleasing solely to the greased channel of origin
A mainstream slope of cultural Vaseline...

Turbulent downhill vat of discomfort and immersion,
    Lies longing for resurfacing and infinite buoyancy-

Provincial Incoherence

Once science surpasses religion's promises,
    With essence to death and afterward,
All preconceived goals and hopes will diminish...
The mendacious teachings;
    Now cast out in splendor and revision

Our time;
We gently let down millions who follow downtrodden
    To paths of promised healing and redemption
Outcasts continue to probe areas of deep grey and inch
    Forward on limbs of spirit and common sense-

The only true one died on a cross.
Predecessors and posterity are pretentious, repenting fools;
Sin after sin
Conjuring excuses and apologies for temptations and
    Contemplations of the undiluted human spirit-

Nature's cravings;
    Human strife and motive
Excerpts to exempt them from the uncontrollable outlaws;
    Pragmatic heathens who make no apologies
Mopping up honest tears with question and angst-
Hung, beaten and made to feel inferior;
    Since It was written
Whittle away the strife; scream and cringe into your clouded hands
Swarm imbalance with decadent surprise ...

Recurring Reverie

Heat flash
Stillness; Dormant
Non-toxic thoughts abroad
Unable to fight consciousness
Alter ego takes control...

...reluctantly you enter;
You see the insular images, the optical illusions
Down the corridor, up the hall, turn right at your instinctive mind
Pass thru the portal;
The room you enter is draped in stellar images and
    Carpeted in constellations of light and spectrum
Enigmatic mirage?
A vivid kaleidoscope of colors and
    Arcane icons of a world never experienced...

Journey deep into the cryptic auditorium
You find yourself enveloped in a wrath of sinister wilderness,
    Where silver horses stampede your vision and cloud your hearing-

Walk out to the pier;
Do you feel the evil, haunting breeze blowing off the bay?

Recurring Reverie (cont)

Look at the amber light atop the whip antennae,
    Swaying dizzily against the current
Envision the small vessel;
Chopping its way through the moonlit waters...

The water is salty and azure
The waves pull at your feet
The vanilla white, foamy crest ebbs and breaks
Bruises your brain;
    Leaving you at the mercy of the sea

At the verge of consciousness,
    Your shoulder brushes against the sandy shore

The greeting of natives clad in their vines and leaves,
    Leave you in a stupor of euphoria

A sudden plunge of energy propels you to a new threshold
Where the island is textured by birch bark and date palms
Coveted illumination;

As you embark on your sprint for the light above the draw,
    You find yourself dodging ground squirrels in the thickets-
    Just before the light fades and the door slams shut,
    You manage to be on the other side...
Of it;
Alone, with only your shady recollection
Awake; Conscious; Lament

Recalcitrant Peasant

Recalcitrant peasant; a liberty seeker
Pecan Herbal Cannabis and gypsum footprints
Snug in douched roots
    And local boots
Lost gems and daisy stones;
Pitch cat days of old

I want to cum on everybody's day; today
But in the attic,
No way
I say-
To grace my play
Wait for the raw, whipped time-
Yeah, then...

...envenom my beverage with fossilized displeasure
Seizing mediocre moments,
    So curious and clever
Surely a sign
Aligned, with dormant moonlit proportions
My envy confined
In the whispers of comforting falsehood
    And cerebral distortion--

Languid Existence

Penciled braids,
    Beautiful As ever
Are you with me?
Follow the frightened beliefs
    Parents stress and pass on
Approach corrosion with struggle;
Give healing a fight to join the wounded

Challenge gospel chaining;
    Its harnessed existence
Write the bible's sequel;
    A true 'new' testament
Emboss your mark;
    Preach to others our constant strife

Thousand wars of religion
Years of suffering, starving, languid existence

Makes you wonder
Rest now;
Criticize the words tomorrow...

As Ominous as Life

As ominous as life, death perplexes
Guilt
Penance
Commitment to passage
True scarred hopeful passions...
Clashing as we speak;
Typified
Dark
Silenced—

Croon to the Moon
Patient spirits judge described hassle
Married to charges of coming to burst before two months;
    Summoned to effect and becoming
Pressured to care
Silent to seem defiantly impotent

Clash naked pipe organ damage
Head grudge preparing to associate media's bleed on
    Responded beaded potions
Provoked crowd vials
Talented minute experienced disillusion
And the sexually separate enjoy themselves...

Credibly becoming reason's roadblocks
Conveyed to play possible taunting, lengthy crossing-
Thousands explore and flaunt the slayed mayhem...

For _____

Not simply my scabbard
My eternal concern and interest
This aesthetic being; you
Resplendent
Can in retrospect,
    Regard as a hallucination
No dominion;
    A mutual partnership
Flowing equation
An on-going episode
Through you I see me;
    Parallel lives
Venial of most all errors
Silent ovation on my part;
Just knowing that we got it good--

Happy Death Awaits

Nocturnal treat for your feet
Blame it on solitude
Rude to change; awkward, stiff and becoming specific
Decadence;
Unless drowned suffered
Set backs in Houston;
    Plunged aircraft drag out
Tight crouch
Drowsy pout,
    And position reflection
Superior medicine, trained dalliance
Chiseled, declared speculation to me…

Living in fat, happy places
Where every travel climbs surgery;
Paints clearly, perfect gaunt ribbons;
    Chic and fluffy

What you always wanted
A perfect day; everyday; today
All the things infinite
Disastrous, curbed and ugly

Relic beauty
Armor too bulky to carry to battle
The burden of all the wrong things said
At a time;
Cancel and we sit
Wait, contemplate
And we sit

Happy Death Awaits (cont)

Angry and unsure
Tight rolling into one
Dots flash, glowing state of all returning
Plastic stick romance;
   Rich and gentler than before
Where it takes you
Good and bad fluctuate from thought to thought
Every sneeze, sneer, break of soft conscious...

Inside every brow's closet corsage,
   Stink power implanted
Children's meat becoming enduring,
   Dying world-famous crying
Happy Death Awaits
As it tunnels out into the arms of disappointment--

Ultimate Supremo

A zygote when I was her age;
Now in wait
Masturbate...

Ultimate Supremo
Drowning babies in toilets,
Strife to sixty plus years of inevitability
Now or later
Birth is Murder
In a form only for a mother
Civilization's cornerstone of life;
    Death for a life to die

True minority is the thinker;
    Complexities ignored
Easy routes...I can't play like them
My membrane struck and punctured with too much
    Reasoning and debate
Umbrellas flood worldly triumph
Forever pelting on my sunny days...

Ultimate Supremo (cont)

First dig deep and lie to everyone
Dumb people don't lie;
    Honest people do
You don't get, you'll never get it...

Perceive lies for true;
Consider for times of passing
Clock flipping to change time
Government controls time
They laugh at you

Maybe the bouquet chase stone away
Flowers and days,
    Find a way
Maybe grand pain don't fit designs
Maybe my puzzle
I'm there and fine
    Find a way

Dictate

Away we turn,
  From all we learn
I couldn't get more attention if I walked around
  With a gun in my mouth-

I got the 'ins' and the 'outs' down
And I am usually out more than I'm in
Poked at and prodded
The ink is pumped under my skin

Purposely deceitful
Conniving little ways
Star Dog bites the day's ass end
Night turns to protest,
  But sees this as his old friend

Wicker basket holds the Headless Child
Plastic porch cradles open roses
Secrets told to reporters to spread rumors

Pulled from the stem
My head from the limb
Keep reaching and tearing me from both ends

(Girls dictate when you're going to have sex and guys
  Decide when it is going to end)

Paleotonic Scales

Drown it
Submerge reality
Don't let it breathe;

Suffocate
Temporal blindness
Hemorrhage of logic;

Fleeting Utopia

My Virtuous Pariah

Images juxtapose through this windowless pagoda
Painted burnings and charred sketches
Meaningless; blurry

Shadowed faces and burned shoulders
Shrugging in confidence;
Defenseless and seemingly unsure

Don't you know anything about YOU?

Dissect in silence
Divide into two piles;
  Public and private

Accidentally on purpose
Gather and gel together the two

What you will find is a volatile combination
One mixture that is sure to explode-
Inside you;
But everyone will see...

They are witnesses to your unveiling

My Virtuous Pariah (cont)

Do not fret
Do not despair
They are secretly envious
　And will all soon point and stare

This moment is turbulent and
　Your bare skin splits and protects you
　From the barrage of spit and anguish that
　Is seemingly,
　Forever,
　Being sprinkled violently on your exposure-

Solipsist to your mother fucking heart man...

Back to the wall; delicately
Feel the cold on your spine

Don't give them the sting from your retina
It is what they want...

Smile
Adjust slowly the trembling symbol on your right hand

Aimed effect above the crowd
Let it shower down
Atop the conventional hollow masses below
Ones without faces

At inner peace
Only you know you'll be forgotten tomorrow-

Bored Particles

Swinging on suspended shavings
Chip away the hollow stranger;
The venerable veneer

Pitted, estranged and hidden
Tucked under layers of tortured sawdust
Termagant termite's delinquency deprives
 Cedar's oak bearing touch
Splintered; boxed
Set aflame to a chorus of embers

Tender tinder
Kind kindling
So cordial was the inferno to squeeze its flaring nostrils
Deflated third member
Squirming to be wide open
Rolling, kicking, gasping

To hold together
Particle board
Bored Particles
Whose ever move is more articulate

Even As...

Even as the elementally, coldest heart
Must once feel
In the most fleeting of moments;
The swiftest passing of that emotion
Detected; untenable

Could it not be more real?
In the dream of morality and isolation
I attempt to conjure;

Dancing in my moonlit life
I know just what I want
I know just who I am
Subtlest of times; a lonely bite

To all personas and ideals you confessed
You did finally meet someone
  Who was truly possessed...

Such detruncated myths
Make me cease to wonder
Shaking, swaying impalements;
Jaggedly stemming into vacuous uprising
Uprooted;
Descending over rolling liberated declarations

Things said
Words
And not said
Expressed with something more

Even As… (cont)

I flutter to jump
Branch to branch
Swinging lines; hanging vines
Trepidation on Valentine's

Land lines poorly rehearsed
Almost honest
Talk some of weather and some of flirt
Sitting and gazing at each other
Until my ass and eyes hurt

Aside from greatness
Generous, corrigible, complete vulnerability
Coupled with cautiousness; experience
A barrier of individuality
All too rare…

Veneer continued to chip
Until revelation seeps out its tender open origins
The precious ones we conceal;

Clandestine to a point of concealment
As if passed on to one another…

I see through those limbs that shiver
Until rippled chasm closed-
I know just where I stand

Even As ... (cont)

Far away,
Through my crystal ball I see
The brightest star of all
Depicting the girl right next to me

Enveloped in your castle
My queen of the slipstream
Your waves crash against my fragile barrier walls
Ending fragments of a dream

I studied every freckle
Taboo sexual linger
Texture; heat; erogenous
Achieved simply through the touch of your fingers

She never wants too much of my seduction
Friction and suction
Urgent, ardent, strong tongues
Hands touch face when kissing;
Fire ball orgasm through our bodies
Dilated eyes as it reaches its peak...

Even As ... (cont)

You give warmth
To my often frozen universe
Without purpose or provocation

Our tidal is thrusting forth
I have reached its crest
I close my eyes
I can feel your tongue on mine
As you drag your nails across my chest

I'll never find anyone to replace you
And I never would want to;
Go through this life,
Without you ...

(To: _____)

Do Not Read Into This

Assaulted on my good intentions
Bludgeoned with your doubts of us
I can't bring it back,
  The ways we enjoyed
Tried but not forgotten, it is gone forever...

I board ticketless
Coerced to stab gently with toothpick thin cheer

Limber innocence hangs dripping from cerulean skies
Falling shadows cast swollen reverberation
Smug, decorated tears flush my right eyebrow
  Raised to the sonnet
Someone, someplace, someday will somehow
Thrive to be as free as me
State of stupor;
Sullen vision drifting towards oblivion

Unaccustomed to your prearrangements
Vices and habits
Falling short and insufficient
Pockmarked health,
Governed by inactivity

Eat the vandals; their disrupting contention
Seriously, I am marking the occasion

Swirling with red fingers
Chin drops, plunges in to the vat
And I'm glad;
Do Not Read Into It...

Dark Again

Freefall from my waist
A denim accordion lunges at my feet;
Intermittent absence

How sudden;

Dauntlessly I heard
Three months of ordered celibacy
  Spiraled into one gulp

For two seconds,
  It was amoratory
Then it went dark again…

The Welcome

There is no heart into it
Death wish thrashing about

Earlobe stoned outrage
Pillar slowly trickles out

Diamond view enveloping a dual
  Inclination to descend

Within beams that pierce thru the blue,
  And sobs that protrude like yellow speed bumps on black asphalt

Drown in a vat of your own fat
  And backwards confirmation

This is the welcome I've been waiting for ...

Slurs and Slander

'O', 'thee', 'hopeful romantic'
Please, spare me of the euphemisms
The exclamations of literary bigamists

Those English fucks who try too hard;
Concentrate on words too slowly-
  Verbs to deliberate
  Adjectives too resonating to sound astoundingly honest

Speak
Attack conformity with a smile

This altruist deems a haughty to significance
Worship the words,
  Not the order exposed

Thumb through symmetric concentration;
Not the same as incongruent burdens-
  So charted and delivered

Slur and Slander all who speak non-partisan...

Wallow in a Stupor

Wonderful swerving
Entangled in barbed wire necklaces

Green eyes,
  Lucid with envy
Contrived transcripts
Remnant fragments of day old imagination

Sweet pale mishaps
I whisper in her ear,
I tug at the collar
I felt the severed cord,
  The spinal burden

Singe with lethargy
A smooth gallop to profound gratefulness

Arrested in outrage
Obscene personified expectations
Describe my potential;
  Meanwhile not denying uncertain cheerful wondering

Sometime in S.F.
It will all funnel into frenzy

Capture bizarre view points and wallow in a stupor...

P. E. R.

Close my eyes to see…
What's behind me?

Sift thru
Agonies and thoughts await

Fuck you
There's something for you to contemplate…

Sexual charlatan
Self proclaimed
  Post Ejaculation Revelation

Gambling avatar;
Harpoon the cherimoya with a blind finger
Feed it inside the dune,
  And stagger freely

Stricken

Parting the red sea;
  Fertility
Reveal the crimson tide

Cephalic swelling
Purple throbbing
The apex drew evident;
  Nearer
Withdrawal was paramount;
  Secession planned
Arrival of the zenith;
  Almighty inertia
Laws of gravity;
  Human fallacy

Extinction inevitable in its absence

Imbroglio

Hazing in retrospect
Looking back to reflect
Awake for days contemplating

Rose dust and overshadowed grays
A mirrored glaze;
An intermittent blink of disapproval glared at each other
Through the back seat eyes,
  And crouched, pathetic infancy

Taut paper buildings crumble;
Floating atop layers of brown skin
These tiny, faint hairs curled and erect

Naked wrinkles and soiled creases
Spilled black tokens and liquid gifts
Fractured mescaline diabolic jewelry

Hissed attempts to conjure erupting poison emissions
  Of escaping inner seraphs
Lethargic guests contribute to my niche;
Expect my bedside-table-top-occupant hollow and empty by morning...

Days and nights
Freelance and privately split
Unevenly divided from dance to dance

Imbroglio (cont)

Watch me chance, watch me trance
Watch me hail the slit from behind
Cunt licking latrine havoc

Viewing ugly changes through distorted views
Traces of swollen tissue;
  Ass hair and blood
Taped lips
Screaming, choked hips
Leaking profusely of astonishment

Tumbling moment of stench and sarcasm
Stinking contorted back,
  Wrapped in transparency
Blanketed and hiding behind coves and bitten cotton

Stabbed and pierced
Broomsticks and stiff dicks
Take your pick;

Tail tucked behind time
Hemmed between voodoo bookends

Desert tongue crunching earth
Choked retribution of my reluctance to gloss over
Dizzy, inhaling my existence

Imbroglio (cont)

My birth retold through passing eyes
  Of sand and sediment

Hated journey
Despised adhesive bitterness
Wretched, drowsy sanctuary of temperament

Rye excitement
Cultivated grains of boredom

Rich hue;
I can't name what colors they are...

Bourbon Ideology

Bourbon Ideology
That's it...

We made out for hours
Dry fucked
I still could not get it up

This cock is sexually unthreatening and useless

So to Lacerate...

Don't you see what's happening here?
Don't you want to?

Frantic, alone and embarking
Speeding through caverns
I sift away estranged glances to plunge my attack

Snip, snip, cut
Lines are tampered with;
Severed
  And left to spew forth

Concentrate on bleeding
Concentrated blood
Grey matted following
I don't feel like laughing anymore today...

There it goes...
Up too much floral sinew
Cockeyed rapture crushes trapeze monkeys in asphyxia
Assistants crumble puddles forbidding retention

So to Lacerate...
Bend lances spontaneously and with diversity

Mock the Freak

My favorite rite to blinking solution
Diluted to apprehend contentment;
  Strife to forgetful visitation
So I step out and enjoy it
The roof particles scatter with views of downward footsteps
Oval shadows hover passing resentment

What's it all about? I wish I knew...
Forsaken, forgiven, forget
I'm in triumph; I'm trying

If I told you every time I blinked the view would change,
  Would you see me as deranged?
Colors, sand and all those chemicals
I can't help but to wonder

All pressing on worried shoulders;
  Soon to be irrelevant
Captured, contained, preserved and shown to basking relinquishment

Forgiving inadequacies
By choice or program
If it wasn't challenging me in the morning,
  I would go and find it
My precedence set;
Now I can never turn and run

Obvious hungering minions
Snarled to deprive
Lashing, twisted touting
No solution but to break the beak
Mock the Freak

It is fictional and that is a fact...

Their insipid marriage
A dereliction
The hebdomadal ritual was growing insufficient

My proposal;
'Exonerate your vows'
'Smash the sacred institution'

How insidious was I to offer my service in her time of need.

II.
Rational resistance to an unwise urge
Contemplating with my cock and not my senses
(her age is but a number)

III.
Vernacular famine leaves us laconic
Trembling, eclectic with movements furtive
Yet, non-kinetic

IV.
Submerge my fear; Surface my confidence
Bottled up strength of liquid pretension
Panacea;
  Flowing grace
Over bearing sobriety
Truth;
  Merely hung-over reality

Claiming Insouciance

Claiming insouciance
Coiled taut around skintight trauma
  To gobble up paradoxical fluency
Confess to undaunted bullhorn confession
Everyone's waiting to be healed
Drop the bon-a-fide bombshell
Cackle through misled pointed;
  Spinning

If you feel best when you're least healthful
The shit smells great on the neck (behind the ears)
You contradict until its bond...
Very unhealthful; very good
Very unhealthful; very good
All together now-

You can't change the past
You can't ever really change how you feel about the past
Not a revelation by any means
It is a strain to recall the cool shit
But near impossible to forget, for even a second at times,
  The stuff that bothers us...
Negative and ugly is so pointed and simple

On a broad universal scale,
No matter how you end up, how successful or good looking
Or radiant persona you become
You can place the assets and diplomas and paychecks on the table
  And smile and point and look seemingly perched on the top tier of
  Bardo one

Claiming Insouciance (cont)

All that paper and pressed wood burns
Incendiary;
  And that soul burns
Never happy or content with oneself

The more you have, the more you want, the more you get
  The more miserable you become
Days are not complete until a 750 is sunk and a tension breakdown
  Is played

Extensive among peers who find solitude much more
Enlightening and simple
At the least,
Less torturous and self-consuming

You brew and stew
You get angry
What you fathom,
  Your head to your neck
You have to come up for air sometime...

You think, therefore you drink
Turbulent and what is the point?
Prick your finger often on it;
  Acute and up front but pretentious and conventional
If it is you; fine
If not; it's not
Period
You can pretend to understand Nietzsche
I can't and I won't act like I can-

Claiming Insouciance (cont)

The world
Sometimes you can't face it
But you can if you're wasted

We're pulled into this world
Kicking and screaming
It is seemingly obvious to me
We should go out the same way

So go figure it
Over a drink and a cigarette

Ode to Ted

The urban terrorist
Scholar
Genius
Envision the thought of it...

I just exploded inside her
He sits
Stares at the blackboard
The dark blue sweater;
  Bloody rag

Vacant swimming pool
But there is a panel missing
Collapse into trance...

We're all out
I can't follow you

My dick lies limp as his anger erupts

Prominence

Uniqueness
Severed and dropping on the tile
Stepped on lifeless conformity
Societal smile; misfit frown
I favor the latter
Play the game they will always win
Sweep it up
Discard of it
That looks better
Change of appearance, not of person
Who are you lying to?

Inside

Served my perdition
Soulless and evicted
Left with only my penance and prospects for redemption
Exiled from within this insular enemy which I call 'me'
Misconceptions from those who frown down on my visage
Speculations;
  Just conceptual garnish for my feast of fear

The thought makes it tingle
The vision makes it hard
Watch as it devours it;
  Makes it disappear
Expel it
Repetition
Ascent to the pinnacle
Inundate
Revert

Epilogue

You have to realize that you are loved before you can live
Inevitable consumption
All we look forward to
Too cynical or too realistic?

Be brave and live
Seize those weekends and travel
It is so short; our lives
We don't realize until we put into retrospect,
   The times we have and had to live

Call in sick, these things are important
Robots we are not
We're people with fears and dilemmas
Strife of everyday life
Burdened upon sturdy shoulders of constant suffering
Live like there isn't a tomorrow
Make every performance as if it is your last
It might be...

Everyone; we are all here dying
I myself am ascending another step, one more motion, towards oblivion
Closing in on motionlessness;
   Forever dormant
Absorbed by age, devoured by time
Unstoppable; inevitable consumption

Attempt not to supercede life, but instead glorify its persona
My unbalance is identified and I feel the tears rise up from the
   Bottom of my confusion;
Certain tones
Subtle, round, falling moments;
   I want them to flourish
Cracking through,
   Seeping snugly in fragile beams of discomfort.
That is all...out...

JEW + GINA°:

HERE IS THE
HYPERBOLIC BULLJIVE
+
SOCIAL COMMENTARY
DU JOUR...
CYNICAL
— IDEALISTIC
— NIHILISM —

CHEERS!

KAM

Printed in the United States
58599LVS00002B/463-486